A Plate of Chicken

A Plate of Chicken

Matthew Rohrer

Ugly Duckling Presse
Brooklyn, 2009

The author would like to thank the editors of
Backwards City Review, *The God Particle*, *Octopus*,
Redactions, and *6x6*, in which sections of
A Plate of Chicken first appeared.

First Edition, 2009
Printed in the USA
ISBN 978-1-933254-55-5

Cataloging-in-publication data is available
from the Library of Congress.

Ugly Duckling Presse
The Old American Can Factory
232 Third Street, #E-002
Brooklyn, NY 11215
(www.uglyducklingpresse.org)

Distributed by Small Press Distribution
(www.spdbooks.org)

Ugly Duckling Presse is a member of
the Council of Literary Magazines and Presses.

for Joshua Saul Beckman

dense and tall bamboos in the snow

show you the mind not used in vain

Han Shan

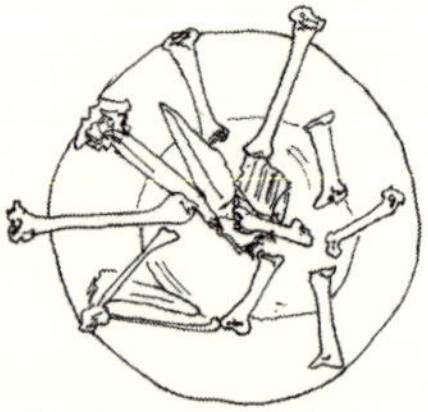

The suneater lies with his belly to the sun.

We have preserved, as best we could, the story of our destruction.

On the roof I hear the black bird blaming the daylight.

There is a hole in the panorama.

I never want to explain love to the animals.

Students actually seek an explanation for my smile.

I never answer the phone, I say, I eat the sun.

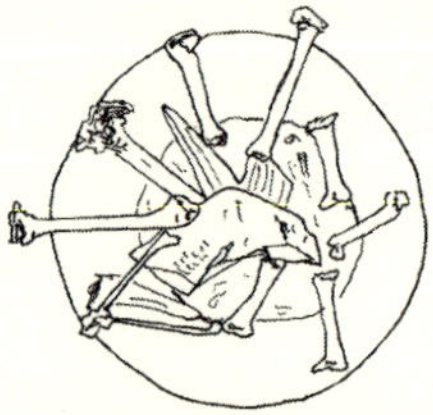

What good is hair?
Why is there something rather than nothing?
My function is to be in love between two people who hate each other.
People take advantage of this beautiful weather.
I was born tall, and look down on everyone.
But I am benevolence, you can trust me with your secrets.
Later, I will ask if I can smell your hair.

I keep dreaming that no one's listening to me.
In the morning I have to steal back my sandals.
I dreamed I ate too much candy, and woke up full.
None of us knows what we're talking about.
A beautiful day turns into vinegar during a song.
The cat is an improper receptacle for our dreams.
Self-love has never seemed like a problem to me.

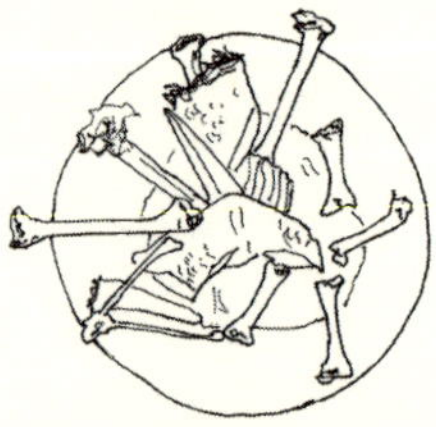

If you don't pay attention you'll slip into a hole.
Don't we all understand evil?
I knelt to the floor to stare at the baby.
Infinite variation in each moment. We're home.
Coffee smells better than riches.
I like to lie back and think of my next job.
I plan an elaborate leap into a deeper hole.

Everyone you meet is innocent.
The day is a bomb falling into water.
Thank you. Your peace brings peace.
Can we sneak a villanelle past security?
You are the word the hermit on the mountain missed.
A cold morning.
This war will bite us in the ass even though we're innocent.

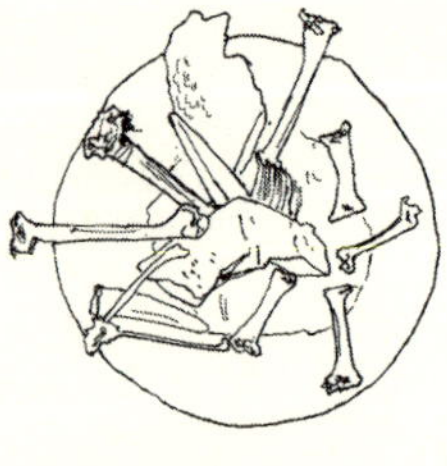

Into the vessel, pour your great work.
Each of you is the universe, though occluded.
Expand hungrily into other people's routines.
Open the door to protein.
Three purple trees and new groundcover in the wet woods.
Stand beside their occult murmurs.
Your friendship is the great work.

Intellectually, I see sex is meaningless.
I think of a beach, a woman.
The sun comes and dies.
The woman turns her head in the night breeze.
Sex covers everything.
When I say my own name I shiver.
I'm on the subway where the mind is meaningless.

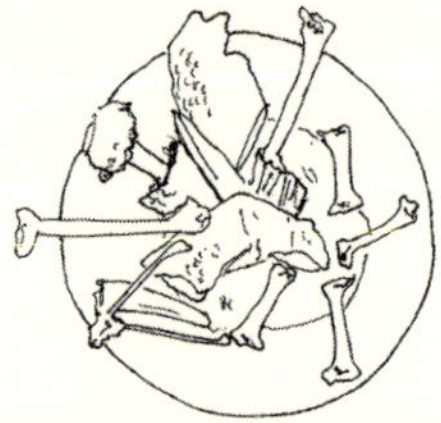

When my uncle was 5, he had a dream about a Mexican girl.
“Benignly crucified” in a tight green sweater.
He was a snake.
People see me as a pale, slender crane.
Dare to board the subway each morning without a savior.
It means nothing to the admirals at sea.
I’m buoyant with years of love from only one girl.

I got radiation burns on the top of my feet.
I got another gin at the poetry reading.
Money, fuck you. You don’t really exist.
I take it back. I need you to ravish me.
Have I read you my poem that’s also my résumé?
In a poem the sun burns unstoppable, like the power of money.
But the elders only have fatuous advice: they say get another set of feet.

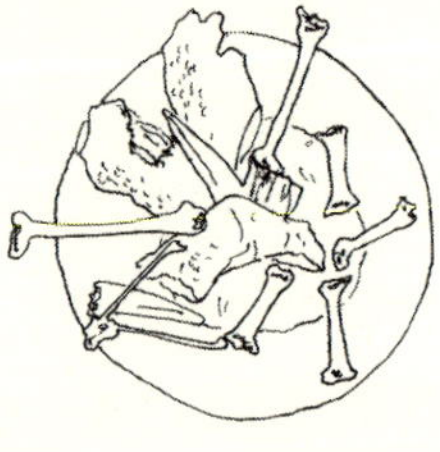

What's the best kind of music to reduce the heat?
Some music is too hot for sunshine.
I cleaned my house in silence.
The baby, X, is on its way. How do I look?
The bell of the cornet will get too hot upon reentering the atmosphere.
Freedom is a big shirt I can stretch out in.
Soon my pants start to annoy me in this heat.

Two boats come to do the job of one boat.
The Adriatic Sea sparkles below the cove.
There is beauty, a sharp glimmer, and no mercy in it.
Turn right on the dry white street named after the doctor.
I am related to the sap inside the palm leaves.
The location of the human mind is less than the radius of its vision.
You must also imagine yourself inside the porpoise diving
underneath the boat.

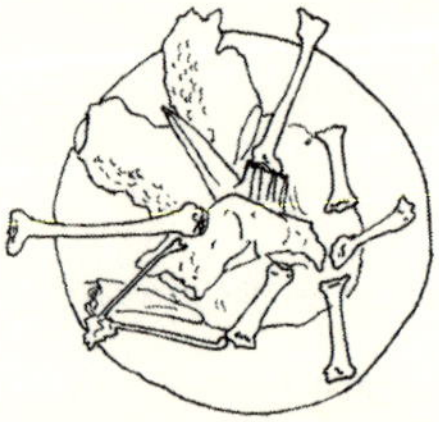

Take your pants off, Creepy, *and be my love.*
Another day tucks itself into the sky.
Richard Brautigan lies dead, like deer tracks.
The Puritans do not want me to read him, or please you.
The self-righteous all smell the same.
They are trapped in ice. The ice is in their minds.
They are exactly like the jello salads they love.

I feel like I really am my thoughts.
Let's see what would follow that statement.
I am also six feet, two inches tall, with broad shoulders.
I am wearing cut-offs.
My wife is a little girl. We live in a shoe.
And my thoughts have run up against the invisible barrier.
All day I have been having raindrops for thoughts.

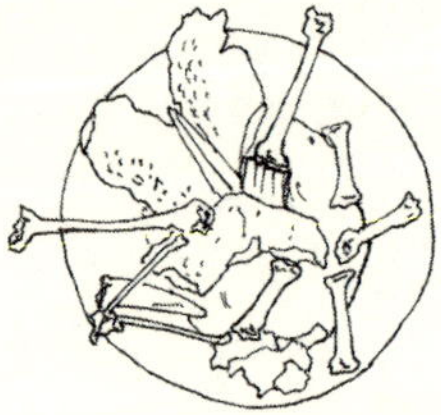

Join me in bed for sympathetic magic.
The little children are dressed up like leaves.
In the night you will suffer all the wounds that were hidden by day.
I know I am disbursing a powerful influence over you.
The bullet holes are still in the walls.
Lightning will strike the likeness of the black bird tonight.
Our necks fit together like two birch rods drowned in magic.

In this line everything about me is summed up.
All I care about is nudity.
Fishermen must never say the name of a cat or pig at sea.
These superstitions came from the sun.
My head was cracked open and will hold nothing but love.
Love turns up everywhere, in pieces and waves.
I like to lie on my back and look up.

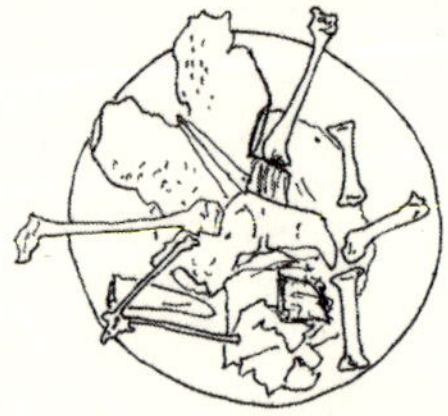

While struggling with a shirt this morning I saw we were
    the same thing.
I am not wearing that shirt with the sleeves too short anymore.
I am waiting for the water to boil for laundry.
Dualism is proved wrong each morning with coffee.
Beautiful legs have arrived.
The evening fills with birdsong proving no one is alone.
Or this proves they are not birds – it's the same thing.

My hand throbs and the storm arrives.
The cow will not be milked by the man who's eaten a tiger.
I did my chores, then I sat down empty.
All day I've felt connected to all things.
A low horn out on the harbor.
I hear it in bed. I want to touch everybody with sound.
This seems beautiful until the whippoorwill arrives.

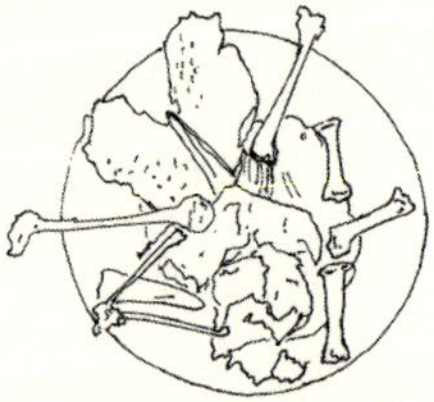

Some guy says Wittgenstein proved there's no thought without language.
Wittgenstein had never seen a bird or a bear.
Trees swayed in the park and their tops touched tenderly.
Even though I'm the youngest, I am the teacher!
On the roof the crows caw at me, and can't land.
I wake indistinguishable from the washed-out morning.
All I am is thought without language.

Grandma looked at the clock and it was twenty to one.
I just fell in the river, grandma knew, she came running.
When she died the clock died in the car.
Like you I won't let go of anything out of loneliness.
A species of red bird was important to her.
Her symbol was a rose that blooms in Arizona.
When a stranger on the A train asks me, it's twenty to one.

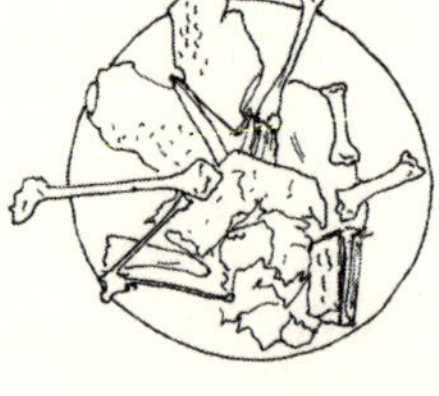

The garbage in the can is hotter than the air.
The heat is appalling and we don't own our apartment.
Humans are really only happy in a 30° Fahrenheit range.
And some people are ugly, my wife adds.
Like a tonsure around the city – orange clouds of heat.
Then the accordion stifles its cry.
I am almost nothing, mostly water and air.

My name is melting.
My sighs are lost in an old accordion.
Why does the moment have to be eternal?
People still write music in unbearable heat.
Animals know they are dreaming.
This line is an homage to everyone I owe.
This line is melting.

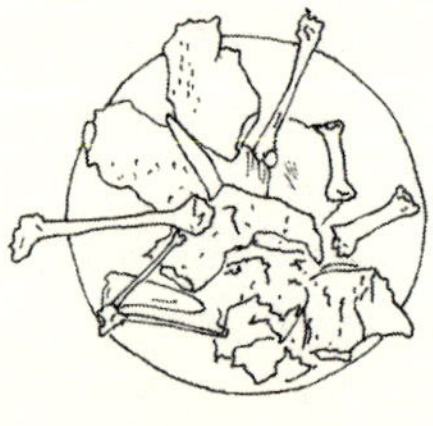

I have one air-conditioned room and I'm going to a movie.
In Southern Colorado in the mountains it's beautiful, there are sand dunes.
The prairie is not boring, it is outrageously philosophical.
Jaime sits outside his store.
Mr. Choi hates his store.
In America even I could have a little store.
Some days I forget we're more than a movie.

I like the name Bellorussian Autocephalus Church.
I'm leaking all over the endless sidewalk.
It's hotter than panic.
It's hotter than *wu-wei.*
You know, non-action. My movie is sold out.
Living through today would be easier in a cow town.
But at the end of the week you're expected to attend church.

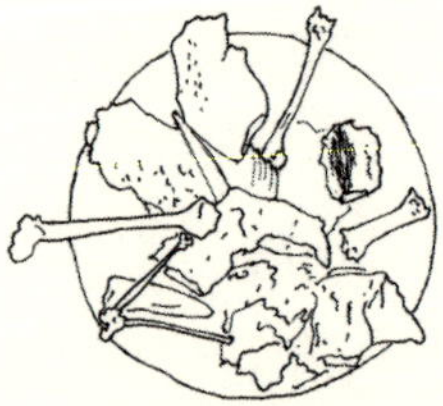

Fire truck along the bright street.
Rosalita waving from her stoop beneath the flag.
Mocked three times by a little girl and your hair turns white.
A hot day in America.
A girl in a purple dress coasts by on her bike.
The best thing is to be very small.
Take your enormous love for one woman into the street.

One of us was the mortar, one was the pestle.
I have my suspicions which was which.
Strange lights appeared over our artesian well.
A woman on our corner sings a drunken song under the streetlight.
My wife is even more screwed up than I am.
She keeps changing into a seagull and floating away.
She is clearly the pestle.

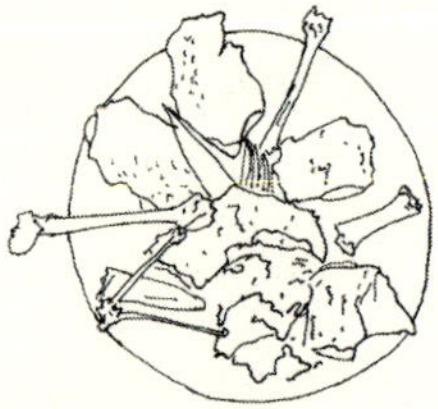

His music thrills me.
He sweeps up trash.
I have stabbed trash with a nail on a stick.
The sun poured down its condemnation.
During his songs I see brief glimpses of my dreams.
The basilisk curls up and sleeps between my feet.
For some reason it does not want to kill me.

The guitar solo in the hot afternoon.
There is cold guacamole and hard cider.
The ghost haunts the rocking chair.
Some people worship a rock that fell out of the sky.
I worship Time because it comes into our homes and punches us
in the neck.
Joshua comes to our homes to redeem us.
There is enough liquor to dive into and not surface all afternoon.

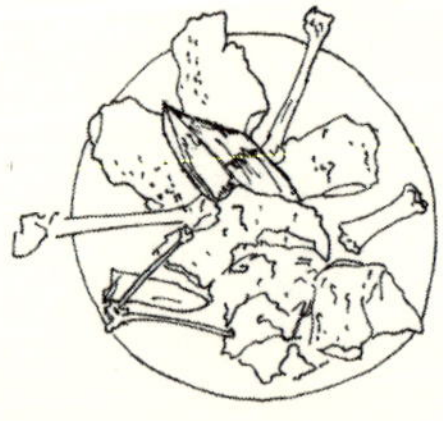

Tertullian was subtle but he hated himself.
It is possible to force yourself to feel joy.
The gate to hell is through the loop of the necktie.
The girl is sometimes scared of me.
When I don't look at anyone on the subway I emanate peace.
Even a cruel woman is no more than a sparrow.
How can the man who swats her love himself?

He gave me the keys to his illegal occupation.
I was the only Caucasian in the court room.
He said "It's well known the ancient Chinese used to parade yetis
through their courts."
He is thin, and in love with a woman on a television show.
Whitman hated his president too, who was a thief.
God really screwed us, everyone has to sleep on their roofs.
Being my own best friend is only part of my mysterious occupation.

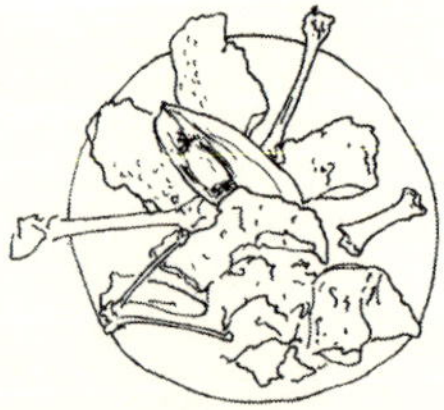

What is most clear cannot be seen through.
The poet turned on one light for a moment.
Empty your mind until you are shaped exactly like the skyline.
You will see green parrots holding meetings in the city.
You will turn to a poem that will consume a forest.
You will think she is lion-headed, *though her true form is hidden.*
She will swell and glow brighter than the moon when she's through.

Having to overhear others is a journey to Hell.
The cabin fills with the stench of money.
That's a lot of money for someone to have.
The moon comes down from the mountains to kiss the plane on the nose.
The circle of my mind is dim and confined.
If I die before this poem is finished do not scatter my ashes in the wind.
I want you to mail them to Hell.

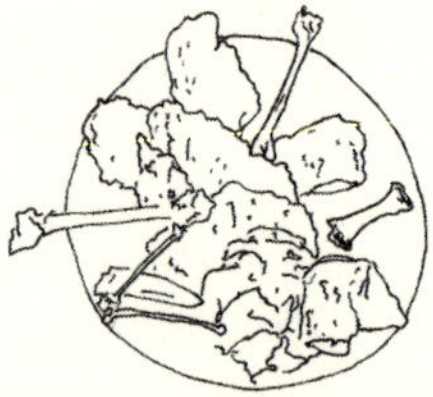

The only English word Marko learned was "distinct."
He lived in the air.
He had the loud and bossy voice of the insecure.
Fortress trains bristling with guns.
All the sadness covered with cheap paint.
Both our soldiers and the enemy saw an apparition of God's mother
    in the forest.
She was gesturing, but the meaning was not distinct.

Lightning killed a man on his roof.
This is making people uncomfortable.
The storm's fury cowed the city and everyone was friendly.
But there will be no occupying army.
I will take up the garland of the Martyr to Curiosity.
The neighborhood kids threw rocks at the government building
    until it disappeared.
Now a bird is its roof.

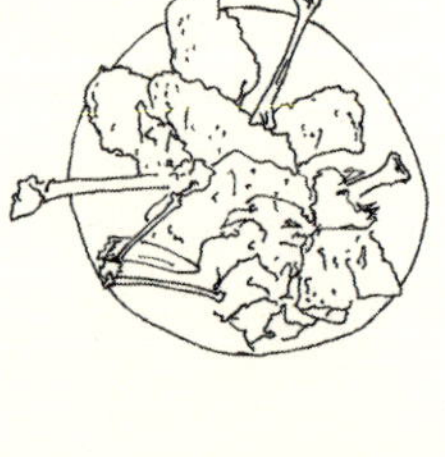

Panting cat.
A white skyline melting away.
This is not about desire.
Humidity like this reveals the unity of all things.
Now all that's left is to sit back and await meaning.
If I don't finish this poem before the pen runs out you know how it ends.
I'm on my roof sharing a triangle of shade with my cat.

One bird admonishes my cat.
Two birds admonish my cat.
Three birds admonish my cat.
Four birds admonish my cat.
Five birds admonish my cat.
Six birds admonish my cat.
Now seven birds admonish my cat.

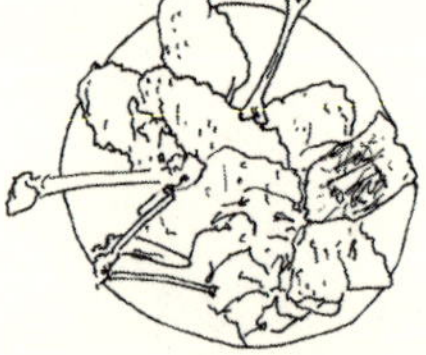

Waiting to be called for a temp job.
I don't have a black shirt.
I'm not "hip" enough.
I'm also waiting for a cataclysmic storm to obliterate business.
A ghost says "grow beans to sell so you can buy what you really want."
Sitting in front of the window fan, I hear the world chopped into pieces.
I pretend this is my job.

The experts looked into it and they said it is all emptiness.
A golden eye stares at me across the threshold.
I would rather be lost in a snowfield than a desert.
This is called "Embracing Limitations."
My head is too full, full of tiny hot stones.
I remember it vividly, where I was, the day I learned not to fear
mental phenomena.
I was driving a Volkswagen right through the emptiness.

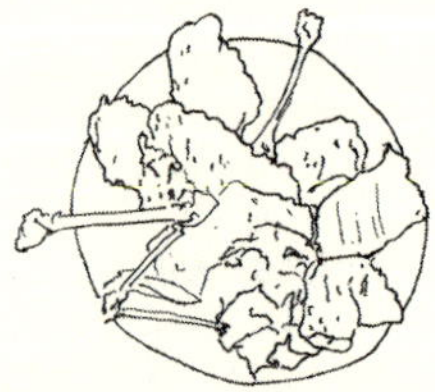

Again tonight I will eat a can of black beans.
I'm in no hurry.
The horribles have taken themselves away today.
I know it is exquisitely hot in Brda now.
In a dim crypt eating *prsut* and drinking cool wine.
Contemplation places all of this inside me.
All of this and beans.

The healthy heat of Goriska Brda.
The dewy plums with little worms.
The crumbled house and smudge pots on the path at night.
Bombs continuing to explode inside people's smiles.
I would take myself away forever to a mountain cave if it were clean
 and full of gold.
This is called "Quarantined Desire."
Figs and nuts and old wine in the cellars of Goriska Brda.

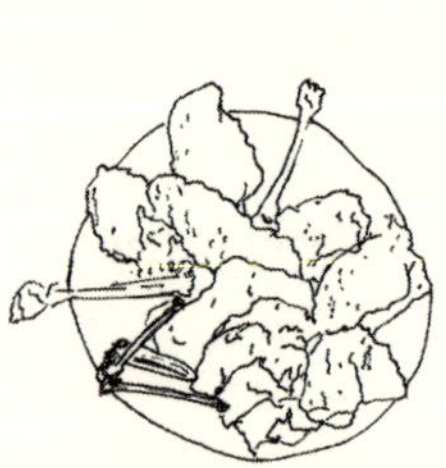

Today it's clear.
Under immigrant skies.
The animals perform the same actions as the wind-up animals.
Anthony, go to the hills to ask a question of the Mushroom God.
All my questions were answered when I saw two crows
    walking to school.
The basement is scary but the roof is beautiful.
I can see right through my hand, though my hand is not clear.

Avenue A, I'm in love with everyone's face.
So many streets are miserable and populated by the miserable.
I'm angry thinking of others, and then I let it go.
I only have to be myself.
And Ron Padgett is sharper and meaner than he appears.
People on the F train are judging books by their covers.
People on the R train all have my face.

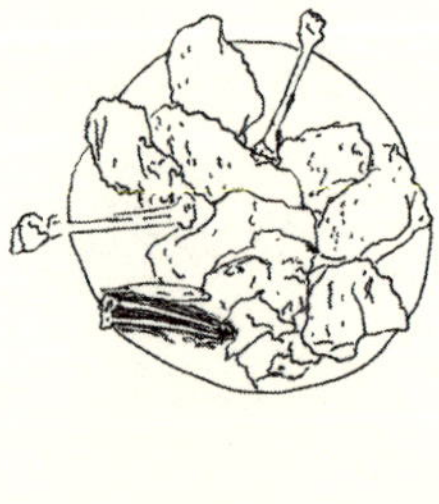

I will never tire of looking at the sea.
Though I am a galley slave.
Drown me and I will bob back.
I can't even write, I have to keep looking at the water.
I came here for glory and was given the sea.
And everything else was denied me.
But my love, she is also from the sea.

Brief trip to Staten Island to check page proofs.
Small clusters of the French and 3 identical drunks.
The city disappears into the sea.
I see the magazine kiosk as if it were in another country.
They are boy crazy in the humid confusion.
The fish are confused.
A golden pigeon walks up to reassure those who need proof.

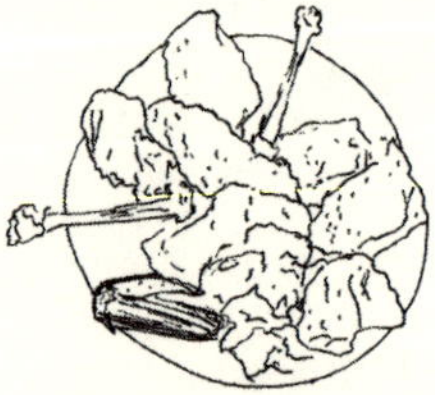

The harbor is calm tonight.
Behind the city is a fog without stars.
The universe never ends and people are slaves.
When the man finishes singing everyone claps, nobody pays.
My sister seems to walk by, but it's not her, she's not here.
Now I love everyone a little bit more.
I will not be laid in a coffin tonight.

There's a hum.
Even to be away for one day is painful.
I will never grow up.
When you and I are in bed we're still children.
We eat until it hurts.
On the roof at night your hair tossed in a wind from the sun.
The trees are speaking to each other, the cicadas hum.

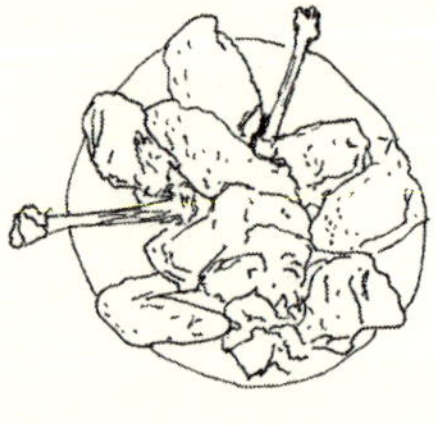

The sun sets into the moon.

Cats switch allegiances.

There is a sled in the supermarket.

A highway in the sky.

I live directly beneath it.

A cool breeze comes from space.

I have to go up to the roof to polish the moon.

Poets do not understand poetry.

You can't send a message in a poem; tell them precisely what to do.

Tell them to cross the bridge, turn left, extinguish the joint.

Do not fall into stupid love.

They will sit out on the dewy lawn looking at stars all night.

You can't kill them.

They have to kill themselves in their own poetry.

I thought of screwing you the entire drive into the mountains.
Rock and Roll is definitely here to stay.
The sky over the Green Mountains has the contours of your face.
When you look into the distance every place else just seems
 superfluous.
But we're using three beds.
I drew you a picture on our pillow.
I am the bird that circles our house, then flies towards the mountains.

What if death gives us no perspective?
We'll continue with the Indian Wars.
I'm just looking for a large flat rock to lie on.
A monk hides himself in a glade of ferns.
The blackberries cannot hide themselves.
My presence on this trail creates tension throughout the universe.
I should put on tighter shorts for a new perspective.

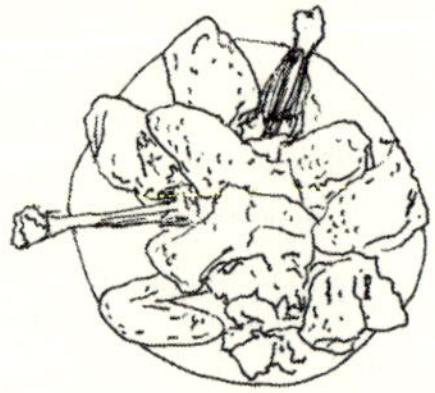

I was thinking how good it is to love you.
I saw two ladybugs screwing on the underside of a leaf.
I'm too simple to divide my allegiances between the earth and sky.
Something disappears on the path ahead of me.
Something else that will never be my friend.
I take up a stout walking stick.
Nobody is around to hear how much I miss you.

I can't stop thinking about sex.
There is a little earthquake.
I wish I could describe to you the gentle rain on the two trees.
Forests of infinite violence beneath a tender patter.
The goal of meditation is to realize you've misjudged your purpose.
You can reach a state where artificial lighting is annoying.
But you are nowhere near sex.

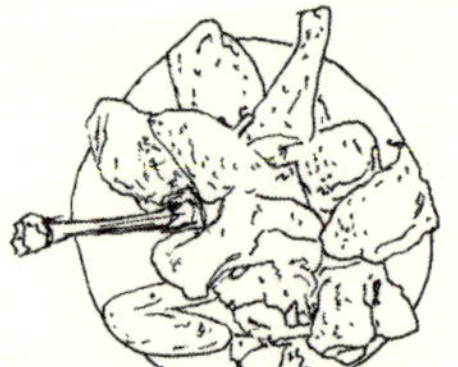

Six crows walk on the beach.
Remember the end cannot always be seen in the beginning.
The baby kicks inside the mother, inside the tent wrapped in dew.
I notice that waves come in waves.
All really massive armies will eat themselves.
The gull with the broken wing will live, but not as a gull.
With her lying beside me, and sunscreen, I will never leave the beach.

Whiskey and Coke is enjoyed by gentlemen and rowdies alike.
I dreamed they handed me my son and he was an Assyrian king.
That night we slept in a tent in the rain.
Two wind chimes called all night in the squall.
The waves came sideways.
We can drink beer in the warm wet wind.
Now all this pop music sounds alike.

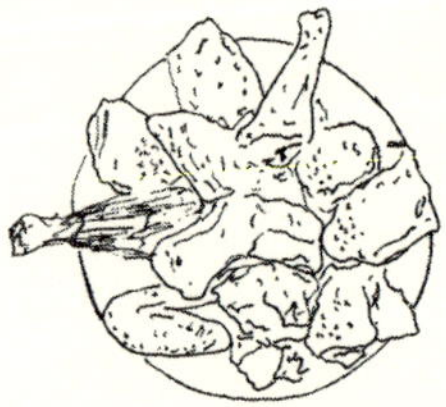

One day the train came for me.
No one will believe I held up well under torture.
And I saw a woman seated on a scarlet beast.
The man in the seat next to me eats cold cherries.
Until the elf-shimmer shines out of the very stones.
The great bodies of water are harmless afterthoughts.
R train limping beneath them, deliver me.

Two people have overcome a dragon.
They lie back quietly.
Pale green buds emerge from the crowns of outhouse trees.
When all hope seems lost, write your name on paper and flush it
down the toilet.
In large groups of people, existence just seems pointless.
Let's have a baby.
Even if he can't stop the war.

New York City, Summer and Fall 2002

This is the first edition of *A Plate of Chicken*, consisting of a thousand copies printed and bound at McNaughton and Gunn (Saline, Michigan), using covers printed at Polyprint Design (New York City) and embossed at the Ugly Duckling Presse workshop (Brooklyn, New York).

A Plate of Chicken was designed by Will Hubbard and illustrated by Paul Killebrew.

The text was set in Century Schoolbook, a modern serif typeface designed in 1919 by Morris Fuller Benton based on type models his father Linn Boyd Benton created for *The Century Magazine* in 1890. The former's research showed that new readers could more easily identify letterforms with strongly contrasting weights and large amounts of white-space around letters. Because of its natural appeal to children, Century Schoolbook became the standard for reading primers and children's books throughout North America.